ALL THE TEA IN CHINA

Also by Sarah Lawson:

Dutch Interiors
Down Where the Willow Is Washing Her Hair
Below the Surface
A Fado for my Mother
Twelve Scenes of Malta
Friends in the Country

Translations:

Christine de Pisan, *The Treasure of the City of Ladies*
René de Laudonnière, *A Foothold in Florida*
Jacques Prévert, *Selected Poems*
Leandro Fernández de Moratín, *The Girls' Consent*
Sera Anstadt, *All My Friends Are Crazy*

ALL THE TEA IN CHINA

Sarah Lawson

Hearing Eye

Some of these poems have appeared previously in *The Honest Ulsterman*, *Pen International*, *New Humanist*, *In the Company of Poets* (London: Hearing Eye, 2003), *El Independiente* (San Miguel de Allende, Mexico) and the pamphlet *Down Where the Willow is Washing her Hair* (London: Hearing Eye, 1995), which was reprinted in *Below the Surface* (Bristol: Loxwood-Stoneleigh, 1996).

I should like to record my gratitude here to the Director and the Administrator of the Hawthornden Castle International Retreat for Writers, where I finished the manuscript of *All the Tea in China* in the Spring of 2005.

Front cover photo by author: a teapot from her collection of Yixing teapots. Back cover photo by Shen Xian: the author in 1991 at Qi Bao, near Shanghai.

ISBN 1-905082-13-4

This edition first published in Great Britain by
Hearing Eye
99 Torriano Aveune
London NW5 2RX
www.torriano.org

Printed and bound by Catford Print Centre

Contents

NELLIE GIVES ME A CHINESE NAME

Nellie must have a Chinese name
But her tourist-office label
Gives this helpful English word.
I like this play with names.
I want a chop carved
With some hieroglyphs representing me,
And Nellie says that giving Chinese names to
                                    Westerners
Is a hobby she's invented.
She sizes people up, takes their existing name,
And makes some Chinese equivalent.
I willingly let her name me, like Adam dreaming up
"Giraffe" or "antelope".
She uses my initials,
Then concocts some flattering alliteration
To imitate a Chinese name.
By lunchtime I am reborn.

Any name is a possession - invisible, secret as Old
                                    Possum's cat –
Both identity and garment, somewhere between a head
                                    and hat.
My souvenir of China is partly me, due
To a gift from the tour guide Nell,
Whose other name I never knew
But whom I trusted to name me well.

TIENANMEN SQUARE

(September 1990)

This is the place on the news that shocked us one night
                                                in June
With the tanks, the students, the streetlights and bullets
All in our houses bulging and blaring out of our screens.

Tienanmen Square is bigger than our screens admitted –
Three Trafalgar Squares wide, and the length
Another five. Mao is camped on it too, impervious to
                                                tanks,
For as long as the living will allow.

Memory stains the concrete of the Square
Bleached as it is by daylight and the passage of a year.

Now children are practising for a festival,
Singing while moving in a complex way.
Red flags and scarves are everywhere today.

Will they grow up to meet their country's tanks?
How much do they know about those baby-fresh events,
Those year-old events that nearly told us not to come?
As much as I know? Or more? Or less?
What were their parents' feelings of distress?
For an outsider, it is anybody's guess.

NANJING: CYCLE CAPES IN THE RAIN

Pink, blue, lavender,
The cycle capes flowing past
Our official car.

Colours in the mist
Muted – big blooms growing in
A moving garden.

BANQUET IN HANGZHOU

We sit at the round banquet table,
Guests of the education authority,
Eating carp shaped like a squirrel, they tell us,
And lotus root, bamboo shoots, and cabbage leaves.

Next door a new building is going up,
Encased in basketwork – bamboo scaffolding;
It looks like occupational therapy
For some recuperating giant.
I nibble my bamboo shoots and wonder
If that scaffolding is edible, too.

They are all courtly men being polite,
Paying graceful compliments
As though the Cultural Revolution
Had never happened,
As though no one had ever been denounced
For being et cetera, for doing et cetera,
And having the wrong ancestors.

We eat together, all fluent on the chopsticks,
Bygones are water under the bridge,
And mindlessness is out of our minds.
This is a new New China; a turning of new leaves.

My neighbour asks me thorny questions:
How do I like it here?
Am I familiar with the man Shakespeare?
Have I read *Hamlet* and *King Lear*?
Did Shakespeare really write those plays,
Or someone else, like Bacon?

I am the world authority on Shakespeare
At this table.
                    "No," I say, "he wrote those plays.
There is no real doubt about it."
The Bard is safe with me.
I'm setting them straight here,
Around this banquet table with the squirrel-shaped carp,
Where I'm eating shoots of scaffolding
And defending the reputation of Hamlet's father.

ONE AFTERNOON IN FUZHOU

The street runs uphill toward a dusty sun
Still tropically hot in September.
Ahead of us a young man stops his bike to talk
To a seamstress in her sidewalk shop.
He is forgetting about his fish in the box
On the back of his bike.
His meal sees its chance and squirms over the side,
Then flopping sideways on the street
It makes a dash for it,
This plucky dying fish,
Hoping a river lies somewhere opposite.
We politely show the man his carp is about to be
A flatfish.
          We are helpful and foolish
In equal measure, ridiculously
Apprehending an escaping fish
Now in the middle of a trafficked street
With its keeper in hot pursuit,
The seamstress watching, wondering (I wonder)
If she wants to marry a man
Who lets his fish get run over,
And the man obliged to chase his carp
Among the bikes and trucks
Under the eyes of his seamstress,
Who is never again going to look at him
Without a smile that will remind him of his blasted fish.

THE AIR CONDITIONER

The air conditioner performs its cool roar
Blotting out the hot sounds
Of Fujien outside in the moist night.
We know there must be crickets
And locusts out in the camphor trees,
But now they're silent for us.
Still, the coarse sieve of sound
Lets in some howls and chirps of the dark
(Outside a cat attempts to bark.)

We hear what the machine allows;
We miss what we know and what we never guess.
We fail to learn the wheres and hows,
We try to fill in gaps, more or less.

THREE RONDELS ON OLD CHINA

I. SILK SLEEVES

Silk sleeves were never meant to be rolled up.
Such garments suggest leisure, as a rule.

A servant brings her green tea in a cup;
Silk sleeves were never meant to be rolled up.

She asks her when she thinks she'd care to sup;
The lady puts her feet up on a stool.

Silk sleeves were never meant to be rolled up.
Such garments suggest leisure, as a rule.

II. SHEN FU ON A PICNIC

> "We spent the rest of the afternoon picking
> wild chrysanthemums to put behind our
> ears."
> (Shen Fu in *Six Records of a Floating World*)

We put chrysanthemums behind our ears;
We took some food and made a day of it.

It was the height of fashion in those years;
We put chrysanthemums behind our ears.

The same was done by almost all our peers.
(We built a fire and got it to stay lit.)

We put chrysanthemums behind our ears;
We took some food and made a day of it.

III. GARDEN PAVILION

(Lingering Garden, Suzhou)

Osmanthus permeates the Autumn air;
They built pavilions just to smell the scent.

They must have passed their lives without a care;
Osmanthus permeates the Autumn air.

They cultivated tastes for all things rare,
Including fleeting odours that soon went.

Osmanthus permeates the Autumn air;
They built pavilions just to smell the scent.

ARRIVING IN THE DARK

The plane has brought me across the world eight hours
From English daylight east through the night
Another eight hours ticked behind glass
At the bare Beijing airport,
And I balanced between one clock and another
And balanced between hunger and sleep.
I slept in the moonless air to Shanghai
Where we landed on the Rainbow Bridge,
But that night the rainbow was seven shades of black.

It was August in China, hot and damp and 3-D black.
Novelty kept me awake for hours.
Our headlights bumped toward Suzhou,
Lighting the road to grey,
Darker grey the avenues of trees, lush as hedges.
Laden bikes swaying toward some market
Hover at the headlight's edges.

On the dark campus a few streetlights burn.
The car stops and cicadas rasp from the bamboo trees,
Louder than the car was.
                                        I go to my rooms
Bright with sudden Chinese light
On my unfamiliar Chinese chairs.
I turn toward bed for the remainder of the night.
But these early foreign hours
Keep me up like coffee, make me unpack
And find my radio, make me locate
The BBC and draw a mark
On the dial to hear the news
Out of habit, one familiar habit,
Here in the foreign dark.

THE EGG ON THE BALCONY

August is the year's storage heater.
All the summer sun-pounding is still
Here pulsing through the Yangtze Valley.
The air conditioning is my refuge.
The balcony is too hot to visit,
Except to string up my wet hand-wrung clothes
That are nearly dry by the time I finish.

I could fry an egg on my balcony today:
The egg would run into the cracks
Between the tiles out there,
Then the sprawl would harden
From the edges inward
And I would have a little dinner-party joke
To recount in years to come.

This is the very balcony
Where a foreign teacher
Once broke an egg and cooked it
Without intending to eat it.
The heat can affect those soft foreigners.
No, not in a pan, but on the floor,
The floor where you walk,
Yes, the tile floor of the balcony,
Not dropped by accident
But quite deliberately.
Li Mei-Ling saw her do it.
She saw it all, you can ask her.
She was all right when the weather cooled.
She did it only the one time.
It was the heat. Li Mei-Ling saw it all.

So I don't do it.
I merely look out at those hot tiles
And think how easy it would be.

FOREIGN EXPERT

I'm an expert – it's written in the contract –
And classes sit at my feet four days a week.
Outside the classroom I revert to ignorance.
The lady selling roasted melon seeds
Has to hold up fingers for the price.
Even the obvious abacus is no good,
Although all over town everyone plays
That rectilinear rosary,
Noisy as ping pong
On all the city's counter-tops.

Banners shout across the street
Messages to everyone but me.

STUDENT QUESTION

It was the one question I didn't expect.
Simple, but it left me astounded.
My Chinese student with the greatest respect
Must have thought
I had the answer he sought –
Couldn't have guessed how it sounded.

He himself would have known
A response to give *a propos*
Of the relevant sum of his own,
So he spoke quite seriously
When he earnestly enquired of me,
"How many English words do you know?"

IN PRAISE OF MY RADIO

My radio's tasted other alphabets.
It wears my initials in Greek –
Sigma Lambda, like a college lavalier.
It plays tapes and catches VOA
Out of the air like a softball.
It transports me to London by the ear
At dawn. Bush House is a newspaper boy
Throwing me the headlines in the dark,
But they arrive in China with tomorrow's light
Slanting through the bamboo trees.

THE EVENING RAID

(from my balcony at the
Foreign Experts' Building)

Around six the bats come over
Like an air raid. I cheer them on
Recommending mosquitoes on the menu,
The soup of the day swarming in the dusk.
Go to it, bats, I tell the airborne mice,
Eat up, help yourself to seconds, even thousandths.
Have some *moustiques chinois*,
Try the *petits moustiques vivants à la Suzhou.*

I think of them fat and glossy up there
Picking their teeth and hiccupping back to base
On the odious flies stinging me all day.
I don't begrudge them
The secondhand protein of a drop of blood.
I wish them repletion and daily pastures new
Where never have so many been eaten by so few.

THREE TIME PIECES

I. THE CLOCK BUILDING

Left behind like an old hymnal
By the Methodists who set the place ticking,
The Clock Building is neo-everything in brick.
Toward the end of term I take
My older class around the walls
And tell them why the chapel window
Looks like that. "This is Gothic," I say,
And "That looks French".

But the neglect is pure Chinese.
The clock is stopped in four directions
Like a dried-up lighthouse in a sea of trees.
Ten-to-three splays across the face,
Behind which lies a cube of empty space.

II. MY WRISTWATCH LYING ON THE LECTERN

I slip it off my wrist as the bell's ringing
And lay it within glancing range.
This quartz sand runs through the class
Startling me variously by its speed.
It's right to second, as the bells,
I notice, certainly aren't.

I set it by the BBC
Every now and then, GMT.

They know the class is over
When I fit it back on my pale bracelet
As I describe their hurdle for next week.
They're impatient, but I make them wait;
The bell goes, a minute and many seconds late.

III. ALARM CLOCK

A good alarm, but overeager.
Every night I have to rein it in
When I'm giving it instructions
For the morning.
                    But at six I wake
And watch that restless hand edge
Toward smaller angles. I am Faustus,
Monday morning my midnight.
Oh, *currite lente*! Hold of a little while.
Why this relentless gallop down the dial?

LOUDSPEAKERS ON THE CAMPUS

The loudspeakers perch like Gessler's hat
On poles around the campus,
Put in place in that civil war
Of twenty years ago. ("You've heard of
The Cultural Revolution?" the students ask,
Not even remembering it themselves.)
Now they play Strauss waltzes or Elvis Presley;
A hectoring voice in Chinese,
And many mornings the BBC in English.

Once the loudspeakers shouted like firecrackers
Declaiming Mao's thoughts:
If you can stuff the air full enough of it,
It must be true. But now who understands
This cultural discussion of Thackeray?
Who, hurrying to class, can stop
To decipher Becky Sharp?

FLASHY PARTY PIECE

Whatever comment I expected
After the first English class,
When the bell was still floating in the room,
It wasn't the comment I got.
The Chinese student asked, fascinated,
Speaking carefully, "Why do you use
Your left hand to write on the board?"
She thought it was a stunt, a trick
To entertain the class.
                    The answer was so dull
Compared to my flashy party piece.
I told her (what a lame excuse!)
That I was left-handed. And she looked
At me with a puzzled stare, then
A recollection of someone she'd heard of once,
Perhaps a friend of a cousin's neighbour,
Who was said to write and even sometimes eat
With his left hand. Someone was supposed
To have seen it once.
                    Once again I see
That unbeknownst to me
I'm as freakish as a panda wearing roller skates,
Infinitely entertaining to the local gaze.
Something about it entertains me, too,
But there is something else that grates.
I can stop the traffic in a dozen ways
By doing what I always do.
What narrowness is this that finds me strange
In a world where variety is the norm,
Where in all our unpredicted range
Even formlessness is a kind of form?

"DO NOT SPIT"

Of all the things we need to know,
Of all the facts and news we need,
The only signs in English say,
"Do Not Spit",
But English speakers here are not
The ones who spit.
They need Chinese signs
If they want the signs to work.
Are there Chinese signs that say
"Do Not Use a Fork"?

WATERMELON LESSON

A student in my English composition class
Writes of "plucking" watermelons.
I explain why "pick" is a better word.
I am always explaining what my language prefers
To students whose world exists in Chinese.
Some days the mistakes are old;
I have corrected them before
But they come back like pigeons.
Some are special cases;
Some have too familiar faces.

One Indiana summer morning
Our young Herr Gerlach
Bounded onto his desk in class,
Startling us out of any grammar-induced torpor,
Exclaiming, "*Auf den Tisch*!"
He stamped in his European sandals
(So European, worn with socks),
"*Auf!*" he said. "*Auf!*"
This is what *auf* means,
And nearly thirty years after that day
I remember his sandals and his socks
And one German preposition anyway.

"You *pluck* small things," I say. "A flower, perhaps,
A hair." Here I separate out one hair for illustration
Dramatically, on the top of my head. "I *pluck* a hair!"
My students chuckle; I have their full attention.
To make it stick, I pluck a pair.

I think of them in thirty years.

Will they say, "We had a teacher once at college
Who showed us what a verb meant
By plucking a hair from her head"?
They may remember this
Out of everything I've said.

THE FOREIGN EXPERT DISCOURSES ON IRONY

I am teaching irony ("Why
Does Mr. Bennet say this to his daughter?")
And today I wear it, too.
This jacket from my mother's things
Wasn't on the scene in time to stand
In front of any of the many classes
She retired from, but there's no escape
And now the sleeves have made their teacher-gestures
                                                    anyway.

She couldn't have imagined the fine snowfall
Of daily Chinese chalk drifting on the cuffs.
I write "irony" on the board
And think a wink at my arm.

MISS ZHOU DROPS A BOMBSHELL

"You may not believe this," she says,
Challenging me to imagine –
Pausing to let me prepare myself –
"But
"Not everyone
"In China
"Has
"A television set."
The bathos leaves me speechless
But she reads it
As shock at deprivation.

THE VENICE OF THE EAST

"Our city is called the Venice of the East,"
My Suzhou student says
Proud of the allusion
Connecting her city to the outside world.

I think, Venice, yes,
The afternoon we got lost
And came out in the little piazza
With San Rocco at one side,
Ancient, ornate, and closed for repairs;
Our hotel up near the train station
On the Grand Canal before it wanders under its bridges;
Around the corner from the palace
The little picnic park, the *pane francese* and wine.

Then the gloom of St. Mark's
And the thousand-year-old mosaic glitter.
Everything was a backdrop for us then,
When the object of every day
Was to spend it together.

I look around now at the low Ming houses
And these fine stone bridges.
Some Suzhou silk may well
Have ended up on the doges' backs.

She's never left this province,
Lucky to see Venice in a magazine.
I couldn't describe it to her if I tried.
"This is just like Venice,"
I assure my guide.

GALAHAD ON WU STREET

A white charger trotting one morning
On bicycle wheels
Toward me on busy Wu Street,
White-skirted like Galahad about to joust,
But when Galahad pedals closer
His bike is festooned with twenty geese
Coming or going to market on busy Wu Street
Hanging quietly by their orange feet.

SUZHOU STUDENTS PLAYING TENNIS

The tennis courts are unrolled clay
But the students persevere and play
In spite of having not one net.
Tennis! Well, how bourgeois can you get?
Were they thrown out by the proles,
Seeing they were full of holes?

The students excel at made-do-and-mending,
At lateral thinking and blatant rule-bending.
They play unselfconsciously in front of me
With a row of bikes where the net should be.

THE ARMY GIRLS

The girls wear their hats angled smartly
And march along on the volleyball court
Learning the steps like a new dance,
Turning sharply on the beat.
They will march into battle
In their tennis shoes,
Their hats jaunty on ponytails,
A corps of armed cheerleaders.
Next week they do machine-gun practice
In the long grass behind the library.
I know they'll do that too with flair and dash,
Firing their imaginary rounds with great panache.

Next to the girls' parade ground
Some retired teachers enjoy a game of croquet.
They've lived through enough of marching around –
They're finally old enough to play.

THE DEPARTMENT LIBRARIAN

The librarian is teaching me tai chi
Out under the October Thursday tree
Beside the walk. Our new slow moves
Fit neatly into last week's grooves
And before it gets too cold
I have added new to old
Until I have a sequence I can do
That pleases Feng and puzzles passing students, too.

The librarian teaches with such care
And generosity, such eagerness to share,
That I feign an interest that's much greater
Than what I feel. My plan is later
To gently drop this impromptu class
And hope his teaching urge will pass.

Mr. Feng is also a talented repairer
Of typewriters, in China a rather rarer
Skill. Again his enthusiasm touches me;
He is all a librarian ought to be.

But then I asked to borrow a certain book.
It was in the catalogue. I showed him. "Look,"
I said, reading off the Dewey shelf mark.
Then we went to the dingy little dark
Room where the books were stored
And sure enough, a thing untoward,
It wasn't there, wasn't where it was supposed to be,
At Dewey Decimal eight-two-three.

Mr. Feng was at a loss, was all at sea,

To try to establish where it could be.
Eventually searching through his file
He found that for quite a while
(For about three years) the book had been
At home on the shelves of Mr. Lin.
He would get it for me, he declared,
He'd have it by the end of the week, he dared
To promise, and he was as good as his word.

As soon as Mr. Lin heard
That the foreign teacher wanted his book
(One that he thought of as his; it had begun to look
At home on his shelves), he hopped on his bike
And brought it right back exactly like
The scholar he was, and just in time
For my lesson plan. The thing is, I'm
Using it for about a week or two, and then
Mr. Lin can take it out again
On extended loan, if he's minded to
(And if, in Feng's stacks, he can find it, too)
And if Feng doesn't care if it ever comes back –
Although for three years he didn't notice a lack
Of this book and nobody asked him to lend
It out, rebind it, recall it, reshelve it, or mend
Any pages. Lin didn't ask him to bend
Any rules (if there were any rules to bend)
He just kept the book and let it blend
Into his own, a fitting final resting place to send
It to: the title, by the way, was *Howard's End*.

PRIVATE JOKE

for Ren Ming-Xia

Spanish was our private joke,
An unexpected language that we shared,
A bridge we made for each other,
Baffling the Chinese speakers around us
Who were used to English coming out of Western
                                                    mouths.
We got acquainted through it, became *amigas*,
And gave Suzhou a Spanish tinge.

What you called the Wang Shi Yuan
And I knew as the Fisherman's Garden
We named *El Jardín del Pescador* as a compromise,
Laughing together at its new disguise.

We tried out our words
On each other and found they worked
Like a rusty key in a locked door.

My students and your colleagues
Heard us talking noises
One day under the camphor trees
And couldn't place the language.
You told them in Chinese
And I told them in English
That the other's Spanish was excellent,
And only we knew how accurate we were.

We stood on our invisible bridge together
Describing it to others,
Thinking separately and together

Of the way we imposed a Spanish fisherman
On the Chinese garden.

Both of us, many years before,
Learning forms of both verbs for "to be",
Never imagined the Chinese/English door
We would one day open with that key.

AT THE FILM DEVELOPER'S

The picture developer is expecting me;
He's already showing my photos
To another customer.
They are curious to see
What the foreigner sees.
Such peculiar pictures:
Only ordinary Chinese streets and buildings
From a standing-up perspective
And some other foreigners,
No one knows who.
(She doesn't look like a spy,
But then they never do.)

The photographer's assistant
Is learning English
And wants to practise some words on me
To see if they work.
"Famous English school!" he exclaims.
Then "Eton!" echoes in the shop.
I agree, and he does his next routine:
"Famous English actor!"
Hard to tell if I am audience
Or conversation partner in this scene.
Do I guess the name or wait
To hear the answer?
He doesn't give me time.
"Famous English actor! Lawrence Olive!"

Everyone has finished looking at my pictures;
The colour is a little hit-and-miss
As his developing fluid is secondhand.

I pay the bill for this
And let the assistant understand
That his new English is intelligible to me
And his pronunciation is everything it ought to be.

AVENUE OF GINKGOES

The sunlight has knocked
The leaves off the ginkgo trees
And lies where they fell.

PHILIP AT THE SCENE OF AN ACCIDENT

Lindun Lu, Suzhou

The woman in the street
Lay under her bike
When Philip found her
In a heap of wheels and legs
That the other traffic skirted.
If she had fallen, broken bones,
If she was dying, leaving orphans,
No one cared enough to stop.
Philip stopped at once
To the woman's great surprise.

He first-aided her away from the bike
To the edge of the street,
Checked for breaks, stopped
Some bleeding.
           The crowd who couldn't stop
For her stopped for him,
The staggeringly different foreigner,
Brown-haired and sharp-nosed,
Taking an interest in this woman!
What motives could he have?
She was not rich or beautiful
Or even well-connected;
They couldn't be related,
But there he was, actually
Looking at her ankle like a doctor!

Inscrutable they were!
Something to tell the family.

HUANG SHAN

We hiked up Huang Shan yesterday,
A three-hour winding stairway.
The clouds came to meet us last night
And now we descend through swags of pines,
Through the cold steam of late November.

Tourists five minutes ahead of us
Are only pairs of white shoes
Dancing down steps hewn in fog.

At first gravity is our pal
Easing every step,
But by the afternoon he's getting pushy.
A dangerous friend, he turns into a bully
Threatening us with what might lie
Down the steps beyond the fog.

Back at the car on flat land
Our knees don't know how far to bend.
We wonder if tomorrow our legs will even work.
We test sitting and try out just standing still.
We turn our backs on the mountain and its silent smirk.

SONG FOR MR. GU

Oh, Mr. Gu!
What would we do
Without you?

Foreign affairs are your domain,
The campus office we have to go through
For most of our needs, and if you can gain
Anything from us, how your schemes show through!

How they show through,
Mr. Gu!
If you see a chance
For something to enhance
Your balance at the bank
You never stop to thank
The teachers whom you cheat,
Just smile broadly when we meet.

You bring our pay on time –
It's there down to the dime,
You're rectitude itself –
As honest as an elf
Who keeps a bargain made
In a faerie masquerade
Written by the Brothers Grimm
Where much comes back to him,
For your interest in our dough
Only goes to show
That you plan to get your hands
On anything that stands
A chance of coming near
For a bike or beer

Transactions large or small,
You're eager for them all.

Oh Mr. Gu,
What would we do
Without you?

We hope they may promote
To some place quite remote
This star of foreign deals
Who all too often steals
In the politest way
A chunk of monthly pay.

Mr. Gu!
All success to you
In any other place
And out of our face.
We wish that we could do
Without you!

THE CRYSTAL FROM BRISTOL

for Glen Lee

The teardrop crystal
You once gave me in Bristol
Weeps blobs of rainbow.

The cool Winter light
Splits into seven ribbons
Wrapped around my walls.

Each day of the week
A greeting in coloured light
Reminds me of you.

I write from China:
"Thanks for that teardrop crystal
We got in Bristol!"

SHAKESPEARE QUIZ

Not only students but my Chinese colleagues too
Have questions to put to me.
I am the horse's mouth they want answers from.
Flattered, I invite them round for tea.

Are you acquainted with the work
Of W. Shakespeare?
Have you read a play of his called *King Lear*?
Is it true his plays were written by another man?
Did he exist, or not at all?
Was he a hero or an also-ran?
Are the answers obvious, or too close to call?
Do you think, you personally, you,
That *Macbeth* is better than *The Taming of the Shrew*?
What do you think of *Henry IV, Part 2*?

My colleagues would gladly learn and gladly teach,
And I am here to help them through the language maze.
An authority by native English speech,
I say that yes, he was the author of his plays.
But I hadn't thought of all the ways
They could think of questions to raise.

CYCLES OF CATHAY*

All along both concrete banks
Of the town canal, parked for the day,
Are bikes in serried ranks –
Cycles of Cathay!

The skeletal longhorn steers
Sleep standing up all day,
Never twitching their brake-lever ears –
Cycles of Cathay!

Saddles await their accustomed load –
Their riders at the end of the day –
Pointed toward home, their wheels on the road –
Cycles of Cathay!

Locked up again at night to stay,
The bikes rest up for the coming day
When they'll take their riders back to the fray –
Cycles of Cathay!

* Thro' the shadow of the globe we sweep into the younger
day:
Better fifty years of Europe than a cycle of Cathay.

- Alfred Lord Tennyson in "Locksley Hall"

DRINKING GAME

Miss Wang likes a beer as much
As any student in the West.
We play an old Chinese drinking game.
She shows me how it works:
Stone breaks scissors, she explains,
But how China, why drinking?
I catch on fast. She must think
I'm apt, a genius.
                We sit at the party
In our coats, as it's December
Indoors and out, but for a moment
I recall Sunday best and sermons
More for grown-ups. Not drinking then,
But winning bouts with boredom,
Our clandestine gestures between us on the pew,
Passing God's time.
              My student Wang,
Glad but foxed, gets to drink a lot of beer
As I keep winning bouts.
For a beginner I do all right
But it's a game of chance, after all,
And when her paper wraps my rock
I have a consolation swig of pale Dong Wu.
The only drink in church was communion wine
That wasn't wine. Miss Wang, what memories of mine
Would make any sense to you?

BUYING ROASTED CHESTNUTS IN SUZHOU

Sweet chestnut-scented smoke flushes money
From my pocket to buy nuts too hot to eat.
I walk on, swinging the bag like a censer,
A steam gauntlet rising on my wrist.

WINTER IN SUZHOU

My house is my overcoat at home,
Back in the land of bony noses and pale, round eyes,
But here the weather is a given
You rarely try to flout. In class they sit
With hands gloved up in sleeves
Or taking notes with woolly fists.
The door-length windows lounge wide open,
Since everything outside has been indoors
For months.
              Cyclists in the street wear furry earphones,
Tuning in to Radio Siberia
As they hunch padded over pedals
And glove-gripped handlebars.

At last I'm one of the locals;
My mere appearance doesn't make them stare.
We are all citizens of Winter,
All joined in thwarting the same January air.

IN YANGSHUO FOR SEMESTER BREAK

The Li River has carved caves
Dripping with uvulae,
As the English language,
Getting to my mouth first,
Has eroded it into its own shape.

We are professional breaths of fresh air here,
But now we are off duty.
Braziers smoulder under the table
At the Green Lotus Wine Shop
As we plan a saunter through the market.
At night we go to watch
The fisherman's cormorants diving
And delivering river fish to his funnel net.

We are oil in a land of water,
Floating on the Li River
And floating on China.

Back in the Green Lotus Wine Shop,
Where Mo has muesli on the menu,
We're talking to some new-made friends.
Caroline from Melbourne says she's seen
A brand-new Chinese washing machine
That plays "Joy to the World" when the cycle ends.

THE CAT IN THE GUANGZHOU MARKET

This cat knows what's going on – that's clear:
Full grown, striped, a fine broad head,
His eyes are full of knowledge and of fear.

It's strange to see this crouching tabby here
Looking terrified but yet well fed,
This cat knows what's going on – that's clear.

Back home this tom's domestic peer
Would be dozing by the fire, curled up in bed.
His eyes are full of knowledge and of fear.

Only a hypocrite would shed a tear.
I've known so many cats – "Poor cat," I said.
This cat knows what's going on – that's clear.

He seems to know his fate is near.
Perhaps he knows he'll soon be dead.
His eyes are full of knowledge and of fear.

The cat will be a stew washed down with beer.
He will never get to be a pet instead.
This cat knows what's going on – that's clear:
His eyes are full of knowledge and of fear.

BEOWULF IN CHINA

We're finishing *Beowulf* today
Too fast, in simple modern English,
Summarized and shortened in their home-grown text,
But I try to compensate;
I make the story as exciting as I can.
Here are the spear-Danes in yore-days,
Here is Beowulf the Geat, the fighting man.

It's all new to them: it's hard to keep things straight
When the textbook's flawed and they don't catch all I
say.
I explain the Anglo-Saxon view of fate
And the atmosphere the scenes convey.
Later on the final they get it, in the main,
But he is "Prince of Denmark", that other English Dane.

I have my vision of Hrothgar's home,
The drinking hall of the ring-giver,
The rough, Germanic, hero hall,
But even now I know
That along the swan-path of my words,
My meaning drowns in Chinese lecture notes.
My students are giving Beowulf a mandarin moustache;
Scrolls of calligraphy grace the walls
Of Heorot, the mead pavilion
Where Hrothgar's courtiers died.
Golden carp glitter darkly in the pool
Where Grendel and his dam reside.

Beowulf meets Grendel in an empty-handed midnight
bout
And karates off an arm as Hrothgar's warriors watch

(Or "worriers" on the final,
But Grendel had them worried, did he not?)

I cannot stop this Chinesing of the Anglo-Saxon tale.
It's happening with every word I say.
I can hear all my explanations fail;
Differing assumptions keep getting in the way.
Beowulf, Hrothgar, Grendel – the whole gang –
Are becoming figures of the Early Tang.

THE SWEET POTATO SELLER

Down past the pitch where the umbrella-mender sits,
The upcountry woman comes with sweet potatoes
And an old oil drum for an oven.
A hot sweet-potato smell melts
The cold late Winter sunshine congealing in the street.

She and her brother came by boat with sacks
To sell in the city. Their village can't be very near;
This is an adventure, a journey
To talk about for the rest of the year.

I'm touched and startled when I see
That she's from so far away
That she doesn't recognize the FEC*
 I offer her as a favour.
She shakes her head at my notes;
She wants the normal *renminbi,*
The People's Money and no strange paper.
No, of course, I'm sorry I confused her;
I put my Monopoly money down
And give her sound *renminbi yuan;*
She beams, for I've understood her frown.

By the next day she's learned that FECs are prized.
Somebody's told her that they're special money for the
rich;
They're a commodity tradable for even more *renminbi,*
And she's learned fast about this bit of city life.
She smiles knowingly when I offer them again.
Our common language is sweet potatoes and cash,
Roasting and tasting, a country crop and the city street,

The orange flesh of the American root
On a cold sunny Chinese afternoon.

She becomes a feature of my day
With her welcome wares to be savoured and sniffed,
And when she gives me a potato and won't let me pay,
I accept it gladly. Generosity is in itself a gift.

*FEC = Foreign Exchange Certificate

THE STORYTELLER HOUSE IN SUZHOU

We sit in the dark on benches
Where the old men are silently
Vetting the newest storyteller.

Mark whispers the plot:
The emperor's latest concubine arrives at court,
And now the courtiers register a reaction.
This whole afternoon performance
Is the reaction to the concubine
And nothing else.

The storyteller grazes the side of his face
With a finger dipped in tradition,
Meaning a bearded man is speaking.
The timeless formulas are recited
And the dozing audience
Are wide awake for any deviation in the tale.

The story was new in the Song Dynasty
When the words were fresh and the plot was strange.
But too much has changed since then
To let this legend change.

ALL THE TEA IN CHINA

Tea is our common understanding.
I buy oolong and jasmine,
Sip them steadily at my desk,
Savour the flavours, breathe the aromas.

I've seen that spring in Hangzhou
Where two kinds of water mingle
But stay aloof.
A stick trailed through this water
Will leave a surface seam
Lasting several eerie moments.
"This is the best water to combine with tea,"
Is what the guide in Hangzhou said to me.

But our Suzhou water here smells stale
And isn't from a special spring.
I decant some from the outsized jug,
The tea transforming it
Into something fresh and fragrant.

Somewhere among these many-people provinces
Someone may sip in unison with me
From a lidded mug like mine
Or a jar with the day's pinch of leaves
Unscrolling lushly on the floor.

I mentally raise my mug to that colleague in tea
Sipping somewhere, wherever he or she may be.

MERRY CHRISTMAS, SURELY

Our mentors spent half the joyful day
Stringing coloured lights under the bam,
Under the boo, under the bam
Boo and camphor trees.
Floods of fairy lights gush off my balcony.
They know Christmas is in December
And English-speakers will demand
The props of myth, deliciously novel here.
It's to do with pine trees and a gnome in red
As politically correct as you could wish;
They know for sure we send cards,
Hang tinsel from the ceiling
And revel in certain songs;
They have all the evidence.

We are stuck with their second-hand surmise.
In vain we demur, explain the extenuations
Of agnosticism, of Hanukkah,
Of simple diversity. "Commercialism," we begin,
Realizing just too late it's their ideal.
We go through the motions for them,
Going through the motions for us.
Finally in March two of us nod without a word,
Get up on chairs after lunch
And unpin the tinsel swags.

THE ARTIST WHO SPECIALISED IN TIGERS

Somebody else in his studio
Painted all the tigers,
Not Liu Maoshan, who did the local scenes –
The Ming houses by the water
All those black roofs and white walls,
The "Waterland" swampscapes.

The tigers prowl down portrait rectangles
Seen from above – the painter
On a tree branch maybe,
Wisely above the tiger,
Muscular, rangy, tough-looking tiger,
Every hair separate and visible,
Stacked against the wall
Away from Maoshan's rivers and lakes
Fishing nets and impressions of boats –
All that tiger-drowning water.

His tigers live on mountainsides
And prowl among the pine
Away from Maoshan's pictures,
High above the waterline.

OUT FOR A STROLL ON THE PHOENIX

The students do a neat semi-genuflection on their bikes
As they leave the college gate.
They slow down, feint to dismount,
But hop back on in one smooth move.
No one says I ought to do it, so I skip
Whatever obeisance this is meant to prove.

I'm out for a fixed-gear stroll on my Phoenix bike,
But stuck in a gridlock on Renmin Lu downtown
Until it frays at the edges and unravels into movement
Like doing solemn tai chi sitting down.

We were ten abreast last night,
Leaving some room for buses and trucks
And flitting like moths under the streetlamps.
The traffic was only slightly slowed,
The trucks switching on momentary headlights
To memorize the next few yards of road.

Today I cycled past a man selling grasshoppers,
Doing a buzzing business
In big brown tobacco-spitters invisible
In straw travelling cages made
For a grasshopper to turn around in
And get resigned to chirping as a trade.

Others' lives intersect with any ride I take.
Here's a man collecting bike spokes
In his front room in a prickly heap
And cleaning off the rust.
Customers come wanting bike spokes on the cheap

Replacing even worse ones when they must.
When the talk turns to livelihood and work
Does he say, "Secondhand bike spokes are my trade.
"I can get them for you cheap –
"Only a bit over what I paid –
"Come home with me, I've got 'em ankle deep"?

Once I passed a man labouring up the slope
Of a bridge on the Grand Canal,
His bike laden with panniers full of geese.
One aimed its beak at my calf, just missing.
(The hazards of traffic here
Include aggressive geese and hissing.)

I'm turning right at the lights
When a man falls in beside me.
He just wants to tell me that he's a Christian,
Learned his English from a mission school,
Had a Bible but Red Guards
Destroyed it with his rosary beads.
He grins (he'll tell his family that he found one
And spoke words in English just this week)
And then speeds off happily,
Mission accomplished, so to speak.

A VISIT TO THE CHOP-CARVER

In a break in the Spring Plum Rains
I bike out the back gate
And zigzag through the pungent alleys
To the next canal.
The chop carver is always sitting
By the window painting cranes,
Pairs of cranes, those symbols of long life.
His canaries are a loud choir
Praising life by the canal with the crane-painter,
Chop-carver, cheerful wiry hunchbacked artist,
Opening his shutters that dangle with cages over the
                                                    water,
Casting the canary song to the opposite bank
Like a silken bridge, visible only to the ear.

He leaves his cranes half drawn
To show me blank chops:
Stone lions, the twelve zodiac beasts,
Polished found irregular shapes.
He's pleased with his shop,
His work, his cranes, his canaries,
His customers, his chops.
He shows me his cranes
Captive on paper
Alive with lines left by the brush.
His canaries are trilling his skill
As I leave.
            Near the door
Is the cage of a little grey finch
Whose act is not singing but hopping.
The proud little gymnast somersaults backwards

Landing perfectly on the back perch.
It hops forward
Then flips back again
Apparently untrained, unrewarded,
Except for some small pleasure, finch-known.
Triangular trip, isosceles effort;
The hop forward to the starting block
The only bird-like manoeuvre.
Is the back flip an invention
To erase the cage?
Nothing seems caged in this small cluttered shop –
This small cluttered shop full of cages.

HAVING MY HAIR TRIMMED IN SHIZI STREET

My hair is pretty close to Chinese hair –
Straight as any line between two points
And apt to spring back out
If anyone should attempt a curl.

She's trimming it now
In this shop in Shizi Street
With skilful snipping on the towel
That was clean last week.

In the mirror I watch intently
Not my own emerging haircut,
But a man across the shop
Having his face bathed
And his eyebrows plucked
And his forehead shaved.

I'm trying not to stare,
But I find I'm barely aware
Of her finishing with my hair.

DOING DONNE

(Suzhou University, Spring semester)

I know these are umbrellas, but for today
They are a compass, or pair of compasses,
As Donne says. See how I hold them at the top:
When one leg moves, the other leans the same
Direction. Donne is one leg, the lady is the other.
"Conceit" we call this; Donne the master poet
Used these metaphors, extended to
The breaking point, "like gold to airy thin-
Ness beat".
        The umbrellas – compasses, I mean –
Are joined, even though the bottom ends
Are far apart. So the poet's soul
Is one with the lady's soul – joined
You see, in spite of all appearances.

And I am running this far perimeter
Myself, still joined by letters and the odd
Phone call. I've better postal service than
John Donne, but then I've travelled farther than
He could have done. When I have done, then I
Will leave my Donne behind, as that is what
Is done by foreign teachers here, the done
Thing, as Jack himself would say.

Remember this example of conceit,
A metaphysical conceit. It may
Well be a question on the midterm test.

THE MA ZHONG PLAYERS

Retired teachers borrow
The pavilion on the campus lake
For ma zhong and tea
On a warm Spring afternoon.
They invite me to sit and watch them play
Their game, impossible to pick up
On first, or second, sight.

The tiles clack jazz-like
Syncopated, but some sense lies behind it;
The players know what it means.
Quick clacks of thick tiles
Fast plastic clicks, tiles snapped on the table top,
Clapped down, slapped, *thwack!*
Sharp clicks hitting the planks!
(A sharp crack like a chop dropped from a height
To make it chipped, unique,
Quite unlike the next chap's chop!)

Intent, the players sit and drink ˙
Their tea from screw-top jars
And tick white tiles
Clackety-whack, slapped on the table-top's
Bare boards.
                    Taking turns, taking care
To keep the tempo up, not one stops to think
But sticks down a quick tile, makes the tiles pile up!
The next puts a second tile at that first-put spot!

And the clatter echoes in the bamboo room,
Echoes out through the sets of double doors

To the crooked zig-zag bridge
Across the narrow placid lake.

THE EXACT TIME IS ALL DEPENDS*

More or less exactness is roughly right;
Estimated precision will do.
How unreal to insist on one single moment:
One second, infinitely divisible,
So even that is not precise.
No: anything depends on something else.
Why pretend exactitude is real?
Considering all the means and ends –
The exact time is all depends.

The exact place is also all depends,
Because places lack precision too.
Places are about here or there –
Near another place
But too far to walk and half an hour by bus.
Given getting there through twists and bends,
The exact place is also all depends.

*Sentence in student essay dealing with cooking recipe.

STREETS OF SUZHOU

You can step on history in Suzhou;
These streets I walk on
Were old a thousand years ago.
You can sense the workaday feet
All along Straw Sandals Street.

Ancient streets tunnel under the modern ones,
Only the names still showing above the ground.
Branching off Hundreds-of-Flowers Lane
Is the Lane of Officer Wang the Horse-Washer.
People still live along Full-of-Twists-and-Turns Street
In this old city, and the Street of a Hundred Paces –
All ancient paths with modern faces.

What learning was here in Great Scholar Lane,
And Scholar Street, and that home of ancient prize-
                                            winners,
Three Number-One Scholars Lane?
What did all those scholars have to gain?
What discussions raged over midnight tea
In Cause-and-Effect Lane?

Does the street name influence people who live
In Justice Lane, Peace and Kindness Lane,
Happy Together, or Noble Character, or Virtue Street?
Are the best addresses at the corners where they meet?

What story lies behind Run-Sideways-Stone-Pagoda
                                            Street:
What legend gave rise to Star-Gazing Bridge?
What history is here, half-perceived,

Forgotten enough to make new myths
When the old myths cease to be believed?

A modest street now is Strong Will-Power Lane;
What temptation was resisted here and when?
What obstacles were overcome, negated?
What character was formed and standards stated?

In Pure Filial Piety Lane
Were exemplary children reared?
Were ancestors greatly honoured
And parents revered?

Suzhou reminds me that my shoes
Are only the latest in these lanes;
A remembrance of earlier times
Lingers under my own two feet
Now in the present year in this age-old street.

HIGH BLOOD PLEASURE*

"High blood pleasure" I think must be
Sheer enjoyment to the nth degree.

"Low blood pleasure" might therefore be
Mild enjoyment of a modest kind:
A pleasing view of dawn at sea
Or bringing some cherished thought to mind.

Now that I know what name to call it by
I'll look out for examples of super delight:
This blood pleasure that's so very high
(Or anyway of a sufficient height),
Denoting pleasure so intense and great
That it qualifies as a medical state.

*from a student essay on health

LUNCH AT THE BAMBOO GROVE

for Carol Strawn

When we needed a break
From the noise and dirt and incomprehension
We met for lunch at the Bamboo Grove Hotel.
They tucked you into your napkin
And poured your coffee for you,
All with an obsequious flourish
They thought we needed.
The hotel was a time-out spot
In the game called China
Where we nibbled a hole in the afternoon.
Lunch was comparing college days
And reverting to our Midwest talk;
Lunch was having another pot of coffee
(No, honestly, we'll pour it ourselves)
And a chocolate thing the Singapore chef
Picked up in Paris.
         The waitresses –
Three times as many as they needed –
Stared at the strangers
Who took refuge in that patch of not-China
Waving off their trained servility
And chortling over things that would have taken
Hours of explanation.
         But we refreshed each other
For another week of China,
Swinging toward the end of our stint
From Friday to Friday like gymnasts.

PAVILIONS OF JIANGSU

Pavilions in these gardens
Invite the lute, the precisely careless brush,
Or the appreciation of jasmine-scented tea.
It's hard now to tell how much has been rebuilt
And what remains of real antiquity.

This year it's all right to have a past.
After the Cultural Upheaval
Aestheticism is back, but so much is gone
That there's less and less to use it on.

In history the Chinese man has been a pawn,
For China is a pavilion where drama is put on.

STERILISING THE CHOPSTICKS

Noodles boiling in a pot under the trees
As I pedal past, a few tables set out
In the bamboo shade, so I stop.
The friendly owner offers a steaming bowl
And, lacking the right words in *Putonghua*,
I mime snapping apart chopsticks,
Sterile and meant for single use.

The noodle woman understands at once.
She regrets she has no such chopsticks,
But she takes a pair of hers from a bouquet
Standing like celery in a glass on the table
And swishes them through the boiling broth.

So much for germs, bacteria, hepatitis A.
She offers them, friendly, grinning without guile.
She sees I'm foreign, therefore more obsessive than
                                                    blasé.
I put aside my scruples for her smile.

DOWN WHERE THE WILLOW IS WASHING HER HAIR

Down where the willow is washing her hair
The little arched bridge jumps over the water.
Bikes loaded with melons donkey-like climb
The back of the bridge then run
Down to the lane beside the canal where clothes
Are hung out, clothes and bedclothes
Clean in the sunlight that sifts through the leaves.

Down where the willow is washing her hair
A flatboat glides under the bridge.
A woman cooks fish over coal on the boat
And calls to the man to steer clear of the steps
Where someone is rinsing her rice in the water,
Squatting and swishing a pan at the edge
Of the greenish canal in the shade of the willow.

Down where the willow is washing her hair
A man is selling rush mats.
He made them himself and brought them to town
At dawn on his bike. He charges whatever
The buyer will pay. The mats make beds cooler
In the heat of July, and the man has made more
For tomorrow if he sells what he's brought for today.

Down where the willow is washing her hair
A fight is about to break out.
The crabs from Lake Tai do not weigh anything like
What the seller alleges; the buyer is livid;
Harsh words are exchanged; a crowd forms around
                                        them.

Street entertainment is the life of Suzhou;
Performers one day are observers the next.

Down where the willow is washing her hair
A corner of town lives its various lives.
A girl tries out a new hair-do and dreams
Of a boy she hasn't yet met. Is it he
On the bike with a new video camera strapped
On the back? What a dash he is cutting as he rides
Past where the willow is washing her hair!

THE SUZHOU-SHANGHAI TRAIN

Threadbare green carpets all the way
To Shanghai, brilliant green of July rice
And silver weft where the water
Catches the light, watered silk
Cut by the train scissors
All the way east to Shanghai,
Where the fields fray into streets
On the western selvage of the city
Where the train snips in
Through the green bolt of July.

THE PEACE HOTEL IN SHANGHAI

Coward called it Cathay Hotel when last
It flourished before New China burnt its boats.
The outer doors read Push and Pull, bright brassed.
It's a fossil now, left to garner tourist votes
Or remind the locals of the shameful past
Or distil our dollars into *renmin* notes.
Ancient jazz musicians in the bar still play
Hits that were old in Coward's day.
We can pretend here, buy familiar aspirin or drinks,
Sit in the art deco lobby and soak up old vibes.
We can ignore the Bund outside – the smells and stinks,
The endless hustling for favours and for bribes.
 China's eternal motto is there in full
In the wisdom of the door brass: Push and Pull.

SHOWING UP THE PANDA AT THE SHANGHAI ZOO

I went to see the panda
At the Shanghai zoo.
He had eyes like a clown,
Strokable ears, and a sad little frown.
His crotch was at his knees, he sat on his spine;
He stared into space and munched a loaf of bread.
I wouldn't've traded his life for mine.
Something in his eyes looked a little dead.

When I turned around to go,
I saw other people who had come
For the Shanghai panda show.
They all had come to see
The sorrowful-looking panda,
But what they watched instead was me!

When there's a choice of two exotic things to look at,
Choose the one who's come from far.
In Chinese zoos the panda's only par.
The big attraction was not behind a bar;
At the panda cage they found the star,
And of the two, I was more bizarre.

REHEARSING THE COLLEGE CHORUS

Shanghai Agricultural College

Xian's choir is going to rehearse
And I tag along, the weekend visitor
With nothing else to do
And curious as always
To see anything behind the scenes.
But this may not be what China's "open policy"
Actually means.

The other choristers are Xian's college colleagues,
Young teachers, mellow voiced.
Now we are all waiting
For a famous person to arrive,
A television-screen seen singer.
She will take them through their paces,
Make them sing with all their hearts,
Take them through the words and melody,
Through their three and four parts.

I'm glad that no one expects me to sing
Here where I'm doubly foreign,
In the realm of Chinese music.
Music is my spectator sport,
Although music was the family trade.
The outside part of music I know well:
The hands on piano keys; the directing hand;
The flick of the page on the music stand.

The famous singer makes her entrance.
Affably professional, she greets her chorus.

When her eyes light on me in their midst
Her expression is something to treasure.
But her aplomb is equal even to this,
Even a foreigner sprung on her backstage
And impossible to miss.

I have to be explained –
That I've come along for the ride–
But even I am taken in her stride.

She plays the piano gracefully and well,
Shaping the keys into rousing music.
I sit with the sopranos like a rest on the stave.
I don't have to add my voice,
Always so hard to confine to a single part,
Like a stray dog happy to follow anybody home.

The famous coach rocks rhythmically on the piano
                                             bench,
Bending over the keys then leaning back,
Her arms straight for leverage on the *fortissimo* patch.
But we're doing something wrong.
She springs up to face us, to explain
With that friendly amusement in her voice
That we've sung it this way –
She does an imitation that makes them laugh –
Whereas *this* is the right way,
And she demonstrates that.

She knows how to teach, I can see.
 I know, even if it never took with me.
Her movements are all familiar
And the work on accidentals,
The let's-take-that-from-the-top,
And the way her wrists articulate

As she manufactures bass and treble sounds.
I've seen all that before, at least.
There is always something familiar in the foreign
And some things are neither West nor East.

THE REVOLVING RESTAURANT AT THE ASTER HOTEL

We go there a few times,
Declaring a special occasion.
There's beefsteak and good red wine,
A tablecloth and forks.

In the middle are:
The kitchen and the bar.

The turntable takes us at a crawl
From one city view to another,
At night the lights of Suzhou
Not looking like any other town we know.

We revolve around the spindle
As Suzhou revolves outside.
We can't quite catch the tune we play.
The pitch is low from the turning slow –
A frequency that doesn't reach our ears.
We're some of the grooves for an unheard song
As fragmentary as the town appears.

FINAL EXAM IN THE GREEN BUILDING

Lu and I are patrolling our English students;
He set half the exam and I the other,
And now we're harvesting the semester,
Meeting here among our students
Like reapers seeing how the seeds have grown.
Now we move in opposition around the room;
We are doubles partners covering the court,
Our vision acute in angles.

Our scribblers crouch, perched on flat-out elbows
Among their debris of test-taking:
Extra pens, a watch, a glasses case.
But what are they making of it all?
Under all that thick black hair
How are they dealing with Adam and the Fall?
What are they doing with Jane Austen and Jane Eyre?

A BYRONIC VALEDICTION TO SUZHOU UNIVERSITY

The end of the semester's drawing near –
I can hardly wait for it to end!
I have spent quite long enough round here.
Today I got my trunk all packed to send,
Full of tapes and books and other gear,
Winter clothes and gifts for every friend.
And now I'm counting days until it's time
To go and writing up this little rhyme.

You see, I've spent the last week teaching Keats
And other poets of the day, like Byron,
That tireless teller of his own fine feats
Whose constitution surely was of iron.
He wrote *sin fin* about Don Juan's beats,
A subject that he never seemed to tire on.
Ottava rima holds the bouncy chatter –
At length you catch the rhythm of the patter.

So roll on, roll on, the end of year!
I'm keen to leave, but yet I look around
And feel a pang of something like mild fear
Of failing to recall some sight or sound –
The way osmanthus hovers in the air
Or yellow ginkgo leaves drift on the ground.
What will I remember, what forget?
How fine will be the mesh that makes my net?

EASTERN CHINA AIR, FLIGHT TO BEIJING

Shanghai is falling out of the bottom of the plane
As we swivel north over the Yangtze delta,
But then the clouds discreetly cover up
Anything we shouldn't see.
The clouds are working for the Party
And they're among the higher-ups.

The clouds nearer Beijing
Have an Open Policy, and far below
The fields lie like floorboards,
Long and flat on the land,
Keeping secrets in the cellar.

THE ANTI-SOUVENIR

I took it with me there
And came back without it.
A peanut did the trick,
Converted my dilatory baby tooth
Into a gap between an incisor and bicuspid.
The tooth had stuck with me
Since it was first born into my gum.
I started to school with that tooth!

It saw all its littermates fall out,
One by one, and it hung in there
Waiting for the exactly right moment.
Long years of my life passed,
And still the moment hadn't come.
Finally something told it the time was now,
As I, just turned forty-eight, munched a peanut
One November day in China
Far from my dentist.

Crunch, it was there,
Crunch, it wasn't.

This is it! The time has come!
I've been here long enough! Oh!
Geronimo!

So I'm taking home an absence –
Not an obvious souvenir –
Taking away a baby-tooth-size space
That I've never had before.
But it's a memento in this case

Of China and something more:
An absurdity of time and place.

Notes on some poems

p. 15 "The Air Conditioner". Fujien is a province in SE China, capital Fuzhou.

p. 18 "Arriving in the Dark". This Shanghai airport is called *Hong Qiao*, or "Rainbow Bridge".

p. 23 "In Praise of my Radio". A lavalier is a silver pendant, usually worn as a necklace, made of the Greek letters of a fraternity or sorority at an American university and often exchanged as a love token. "VOA" is Voice of America, a short-wave radio service. "Bush House" is the London headquarters of the BBC overseas services.

p.46 "Huang Shan". Huang Shan ("Yellow Mountain") is a much-climbed sacred mountain in Anhui Province.

p. 59 "The Sweet Potato Seller". The *renminbi yuan*, literally "people's money", is the normal unit of currency in the People's Republic of China and in the early 90s still could not be exchanged for foreign currency. Foreign Exchange Certificates were negotiable currency that could be exchanged for foreign currency and were therefore more desired. Foreign workers were sometimes paid in a combination of both forms of currency.

p. 61 "The Storyteller House in Suzhou". The Song Dynasty lasted from 960 to 1279.

p. 64. "The Artist Who Specialised in Tigers". Liu Maoshan (1942-) is a distinguished artist known for his atmospheric watercolours depicting scenes of the lakes, waterways, and ancient villages around Suzhou in southern Jiangsu Province.

p. 78 "Pavilions of Jiangsu". Jiangsu Province is in east-central China; Nanjing and Suzhou are both in Jiangsu.

p. 79 "Sterilising the Chopsticks". *Putonghua*, literally "common language", used as an alternative name for the Mandarin dialect, the standard version of Chinese.

p. 83 "The Peace Hotel in Shanghai". Noel Coward wrote *Private Lives* in 1930 while staying at the Cathay Hotel and recovering from flu. The Bund is a boulevard along the Huang Pu River.

Hearing Eye Publications in 2004–06

FROM COOKIE TO WITCH Leah Fritz
With woodcuts by Emily Johns:
£9   ISBN: 1 870841 97 2

FRIENDS IN THE COUNTRY Sarah Lawson
£3   ISBN: 1 870841 08 5

NAMASTE: NEPAL POEMS William Oxley
£6.50   ISBN: 1 870841 95 6

PODDING PEAS Valeria Melchioretto
£3   ISBN: 1 870841 54 9

PRAGUE WINTER Gerda Mayer
£8.95   ISBN: 1 870841 12 3

BLACK FLAME Sara Boyes
£3   ISBN: 1 870841 25 5

ODD BEHAVIOUR Paul Birtill
£3   ISBN: 1 870841 51 4

ACCESS BOLD AS LOVE Ray Willmott
£3   ISBN: 1 870841 47 6

THE SORCERER'S ARC June English
£6.95   ISBN: 1 870841 09 3

THE USHER'S TORCH Linda Rose Parkes
£6.95   ISBN: 1 870841 98 0

SONGS FROM THE FLATS Anna Robinson
£3   ISBN: 1 905082 01 0

SARDINIA WITHOUT LAWRENCE Nigel Foxell
£7.95   ISBN: 1 870841 86 7

WIDE SKIES, SALT AND BEST BITTER Peter Phillips
£6.95   ISBN: 1 905082 03 7

HOME, BLOODY HOME Miroslav Jancic
£9.99   ISBN: 1 905082 05 3

MIXED CONCRETE Johannes Kerkhoven
£9.99   ISBN: 1 905082 06 1

THE CEDAR FOREST Jane Elder
£9   ISBN: 1 905082 00 2

BROWN LINOLEUM GREEN LAWNS
Peter Campbell
£6.00   ISBN: 1 905082 04 5

SAYLING THE BABEL Hylda Sims
£9.99   ISBN: 1 905082 07 X

SAHARA Adrian Brown
With pictures by Emily Johns
£7   ISBN 1 905082 14 2

For information about forth-
coming publications, or our cat-
alogue of books (1987-2003),
please send an SSAE. All orders
are attended to by return of
post. You may also like to see
our new website where you can
order all our books online.

Hearing Eye, Box 1,
99 Torriano Avenue,
London, NW5 2RX
www.hearingeye.org
Tel: 0207 267 2751
books@hearingeye.org

Paper-cut by Emily Johns

We are grateful for assistance from Arts Council England, London.